Teesdale

A Second Selection

IN OLD PHOTOGRAPHS

'09

Teesdale
A Second Selection

IN OLD PHOTOGRAPHS

PARKIN RAINE

Alan Sutton Publishing Limited
Phoenix Mill · Far Thrupp · Stroud
Gloucestershire

First Published 1994

Copyright © Parkin Raine, 1994

British Library Cataloguing in Publication Data.
A catalogue record for this book is available from
the British Library.

ISBN 0-7509-0799-1

Typeset in 9/10 Sabon.
Typesetting and origination by
Alan Sutton Publishing Limited.
Printed in Great Britain by
Hartnolls, Bodmin, Cornwall.

> *With gratitude to three schoolmasters:*
> *Boss Wilk, Old Bentley and Doc Watters*

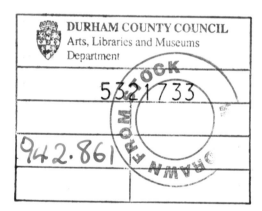
Cover photograph: Galgate, *c.* 1885. This picture enabled Durham County Council to reproduce the lamp correctly when they restored the fountain (the Pant). Furthermore, the sheep are of more than passing interest since it is not proving easy to be certain of the breed. We know from the descendants of the farmer, seen leaning on his stick, that he kept some Wensleydales, now a very rare breed. The finer points of breed definition, skin colour for instance, do not necessarily show up on a photo; on the other hand factors may show which indicate variation in a breed. The Rare Breeds Survival Trust are interested in this type of picture even though it gave their Director, Lawrence Alderson, who was brought up on a Teesdale sheep farm, a bit of a challenge.

Contents

Introduction

Another book of pictures of Teesdale, or any other area for that matter? Earlier volumes are out of print; the publishers suggested another volume; another generation of readers has arrived; a few more photographs have turned up; whatever the reason it seems that the book of old photographs is set to run and run.

The contents of a family album, or biscuit tin, because it is there that many snaps are kept, provide tremendous variety, not least in the quality of the print. The selection of subject matter by the person who took the picture in the first place gives a good idea of the sense of values and priorities of a family. The preservation of childhood comes way out top, then probably a record of friendships, that day by the river, in the Lakes, or at the seaside. Most of these photographs, however, hold little interest outside the family. One event seems

St Mary's Parish Church, Barnard Castle. This tower was replaced by the present one in 1873–4. Note the timber buttresses and the small door into the base of the tower; the main north door and porch have been converted to a cleaners' store. My thanks go to the Revd P.W. Lind-Jackson for permission to copy this picture.

not to have brought the amateur camera out: almost all the early, say pre-1920s, wedding photographs seem to be the work of professionals. It may be that the box Brownie was just too awkward to carry with your best suit on, or with only a tiny fashion handbag, and no motor car handy to get rid of the camera.

Another group largely missing from family albums is what the camera club would call 'Architecture and Record'. After all, the castle would still be there next week. It has been left to some of the early professionals to provide us with this type of picture. There is, however, one priceless exception to this statement, and that is where the background to a family picture has given us the only known picture of a building or scene. The tiny (and pretty poor) viewfinder of the early camera was in fact a perverse help here, and the point at which Kodak had focused the camera, about 10 ft, also meant that the background was usually reasonably sharp, more so than the main object of the photograph sometimes. I have a few pictures of parts of Barnard Castle which are of this type.

The content of the photographs can be split into a few categories. First there are purely family records which often give a glimpse of clothing standards of a particular class and period, so long as the back of the print gives at least the name of the person portrayed. Another group records events that the family was involved in, a hayfield scene, say, or a procession. In this group, location and date are very useful. We then find a few 'newsworthy' pictures, taken not by a news cameraman but by someone who lived nearby and had an exposure left in the camera.

The majority of pictures of places come down to us as postcards, and fortunately the early postcard was a silver image print, rather than a product of the printer where it would have been made up of a dot pattern. Thus it is capable of enlargement when copied. Long after the modern postcard became available we could still buy photographic paper already printed on the reverse with address, message and stamping position. A shop developing and printing amateur films could produce half a dozen copies of a favourite picture ready to put a stamp on and drop in the letter box.

It may be worth bearing in mind that until George Eastman introduced the roll film in 1891, photography was confined to professionals and a very few amateurs. An early photographer, who often called himself a photographic artist, in fact needed to be a cross between a chemist, an engineer and a carthorse. In inventing the roll film and introducing it with the phrase 'You press the button and we do the rest', Eastman brought the camera to the lay person. But it was expensive. If we consider the price of an early box camera, and a labourer's wage, then there would not have been many cameras in the poorer households, and there was still the film to buy and process. The pictures which come down to us are not necessarily a very balanced representation of years gone by.

The camera can take us back to 1839, though the earliest pictures to turn up in Teesdale so far only take us back to the 1860s, and there are very few of those. 1864 brings Elijah Yeoman to the area. He has left a superb set of pictures taken over about fifty years, but sadly we only have prints. There are various tales of what happened to his negatives, usually involving council refuse or similar fates.

The local weekly paper, the *Teesdale Mercury*, is almost as old as photography, but only for the last thirty or so years have they been able to record easily with the camera. Before that the technology of block-making, even taking and developing the print, was just not on in a small weekly newspaper office. The photographs they included were of the occasional wedding, a new chairman of the Council, a portrait of a deceased worthy, maybe one photograph of a procession or memorial unveiling. Nowadays, Jim MacTaggart can be seen all over the dale with notebook, pencil, and camera, the result being a dozen or so pictures of the past week's events in most editions. The local daily, the *Northern Echo*, got a photographer out into the dale rather earlier and had the block-making capabilities. Their practice of selling glossies has meant good prints are found around the dale; the Tees Valley Beagles set on pages 52 and 53 are an example.

In a rural area like Teesdale there is a continuity of families, particularly in the main industry of the area, farming. The second half of the twentieth century has brought twentieth-century industries, particularly Glaxo, and a large young offenders' institution. Both have added a wealth of skill, expertise and personality to the area, with an influx of people who are putting down roots in the dale. I spoke to someone only a week ago who didn't know there was a Methodist chapel in Newgate. There isn't, but the building was only pulled down a couple of years ago, and the last service held about fifteen years ago. To someone who arrived in the dale only yesterday, a photograph taken a fortnight ago is history.

My interest in old local photographs arose when I came across a couple of prints of my grandparents' wedding day in 1900, of which more later. Like Topsy, the interest and the collection 'just growed', and carried on growing until Topsy needed that twentieth-century horror, the computer, to keep some sort of order.

This fact brings me to a final few points in presenting this collection of copy prints. The computer's memory, and/or the floppy disc which goes with it, are, like the video camera's tape, a pretty unstable way of preserving a picture. Either can be wiped out by a small boy with a magnet, or simply by pressing a wrong button. The simple snapshot, particularly in black and white, where the image is based on silver rather than dyes, may well prove to be the best way of recording an image for posterity, almost as good as ink on paper. Furthermore, in fifty years' time, when the boardrooms of industry decide it is no longer profitable, never mind useful, to continue making spares for highly sophisticated equipment which has gone out of fashion, you will not even be able to view your video tape. But at least you will be able to look at a snapshot (if it hasn't faded) as soon as the sun rises over the eastern horizon. That very sunshine helped create the earliest photos, before the electric light, in the first place.

Finally a couple of requests: please sit down one evening with a soft lead pencil and lightly write on the back of your family photographs, who or what and where and when. If you no longer want them, then instead of just putting them in the bin see if there is someone who can give a second opinion as to whether there might not be some worth keeping, even outside the family. I have found the odd gem for some reason or other in almost every album or box of snaps I have looked through.

Parkin Raine, 1994

SECTION ONE

To Begin at the Beginning

Family photographs are at the core of any family album; if a scenic shot was taken it was probably just to finish the film. My interest in pictures of old Teesdale started when I came across a couple of pictures taken on my grandparents' wedding day.

An important day for a family which had been in Teesdale since the Middle Ages: 3 July 1900. The Raines had been on the same farm for three hundred years. The bride and groom are shown with his parents, his brothers and sisters and their spouses. The only unmarried one on that day, holding the dog on the left, is playing the fiddle in the picture on page 11, taken that evening at West Pasture in Lunedale, the groom's home. To have the pair of pictures of the day is surely unique.

The little girl in the lower picture was to become the bride in the picture above. She is photographed with her grandmother, whom we only know as 'Grannie Cronckley'; but my great-great-grandmother must have remembered the young Princess Victoria becoming queen.

Another family portrait which has some interest beyond the family. Barnard Castle is justly famous for the Bowes Museum. There are of course pictures of John and Josephine Bowes, and there are pictures of Joseph Kyle who built it. There are precious few of the men who worked on it. John Hunter, here with his wife Mary Ann, was joiner when it was built. This portrait has another interest in that it is one of the very few portraits by Elijah Yeoman taken away from the studio. The reason must be that it was taken in the back yard of No. 1 Marshall Street, which John had just built as his family home. (Elijah also lived in Marshall Street when he first appeared in the 1871 census.)

Not the Raines this time, but a family portrait with a significance beyond the main event. It shows the new Mr and Mrs Clarence Gray on 31 August 1934. They must be one of the last couples to have used the centuries-old way out of Barnard Castle Church on to The Bank. The cobbles Elsie is having trouble with in her bridal slippers are still there, but since the remodelling of the church precincts in 1934 and again in the 1950s, her car could now get right to the church door.

When the Cooper family took a photograph of June, they little thought they might be taking the only known photograph of the spring which used to be in the middle of the Demesnes at Barnard Castle.

One of the first people in Teesdale to start collecting old photographs, or copies of them, was Fred Nevison. His collection is now in the Bowes Museum. Among them are a few prints taken when some of the domestic buildings of Egglestone Abbey were still standing. The Victorians appear to have tidied the site up more than a little. Here are a couple of pictures from that set. The notice board says: 'Persons are not allowed to take refreshments or to dance within the fence surrounding the ruins of Eggleston Abbey. By Order Jas Scott.'

Mainly Horses

Paid for Catching my 'Oss: 6*d*.

R.S. Surtees
'Jorrocks'

I suspect our local doctors would be quietly very pleased to visit their patients like this, so long as it was not a winter night. There is style here that a motor car will never have. This is Dr Robinson, who lived at Sherwood in Green Lane, Barnard Castle, setting out for home visits at the beginning of the century.

Diversification for farmers is nothing new. Here, between the wars, we see Mr J.W. Hodgson of Cotherstone. He was taking a group of tourists out for a ride, possibly a picnic. Here in Middleton he may be half way round the route.

The classic butcher's cart, with a spring balance weighing machine – no need to worry about levelling every time he stopped. The sliding hood gave a little protection from the weather when serving a customer. No hot and cold, no refrigeration, no lights, no brakes, but Roy Walton appeared at the same time every week in Hunderthwaite with the meat.

The Jones family ran a fruit and vegetable shop in Newgate, Barnard Castle, for most of the first half of the century. (How many of you remember buying a halfpenny carrot, already washed, on the way to school?) The family also gave a travelling shop service round the town and for a short distance beyond. The only people today following in the worthy footsteps of Messrs Walton and Jones and many others must be the young ladies of the County Library Service. Good on 'em.

1907 was towards the end of the horse era. Farmer's Glory, a Clydesdale stallion owned by Mr J.E. Close of Bowes, was brought to the castle gate at Barnard Castle for a photocall, to go along with the card detailing his pedigree and route: Monday, Greta Bridge; Tuesday, Winston; Wednesday, Barney; Thursday, Wolsingham; Friday, Hamsterley; Saturday, Cotherstone and home. This is not the complete itinerary, so it was obviously a pretty hectic week. The service fee was £2, with a groom's fee of 2s 6d.

Obviously a gorgeous snowy day in Upper Teesdale, c. 1929. Thomas Ireland was the postman in the district, seen here with some of his customers, Reg Wearmouth, Emily Tallentire and Joshua Beadle. It can't have been much fun with all that snow coming down, in a howling blizzard.

The horse and the various items of equipment it hauled had one great advantage over the motor vehicle. It lent itself to decoration in a carnival to a far greater extent than, say, a Ford Transit. This is the Middleton Co-op entry in the 1907 May procession. The picture also shows the enterprise of the Middleton photographer, Sinclair. He must have taken, processed and sold the print within a few hours, since the message on the reverse refers to the store team in the procession. It was postmarked 7.45 p.m. Darlington on the same day and sent to a lady in Bedale. Not many photographers today would attempt that rate of work.

The twice-yearly horse fair in Galgate survived until the 1940s. This picture was taken in the 1930s.

Timber extraction was probably the roughest work carthorses faced, and they were usually working in the poorest and most trackless land. Here is a team pulling a load across the Tees at Cotherstone during the First World War. The suspension bridge is in the background. It takes little imagination to think what that river bed was like. The knacker's yard was probably not very far off for these horses.

There is no spreading chestnut tree, but Wilfred Parkin, on the horse in this picture of Mickleton blacksmith's, is still in the village almost eighty years later. The blacksmith on the right is Bob Lowe; the surname of Gilbert in the middle escapes Wilfred for the minute. Would a wee half in The Blacksmith's Arms jog his memory? For this blacksmith's shop, where I had metal runners put on my sledge over fifty years ago, is now one of the two village pubs.

SECTION THREE

On Your Bike

The blacksmith's shop was also capable of a pushbike repair. The bicycle is almost contemporary with the camera. There were at least four shops in Barnard Castle selling bicycles and one at least in Middleton. The main carnival weekend in Barnard Castle started as the North Eastern Cyclists' Meet.

No one would put his car in a village procession, because the poor thing would probably get scratched. The bicycle was a different matter. Here we have a Middleton group, in Wesley Terrace, ready for a coronation cycle parade.

One of the Barney cycle shops, now a betting shop, in Galgate. Obviously a mark of respect for the day of the penny-farthing, but the internal combustion engine is creeping in.

The phrase 'Not many of you know that', which really belongs to someone I cannot remember, is frequently applicable to old photographs. The Teesdale Wanderers Club in Barnard Castle is now a small snooker club, keeping going without the assistance of a bar, believe it or not. I didn't realize, until a friend told me that they had a few photographs on the wall which I might care to copy, that they started life as the Teesdale Wanderers Cycling Club. Did you? Here they are on the Scar Top. Bill Cummins, who you can see around Barney every day on his bike, tells me that since they are pneumatic-tyred, diamond-framed machines with brakes directly on the tyre, the photograph must date from about 1896.

The town postmen still use a few pushbikes, but the rural deliveries are now all done by van. Here we see the Winston posties, probably between the wars. Now all their work will be done by one man on four wheels.

The present-day Whit Weekend Meet in Barnard Castle has developed from the North Eastern Cyclists Meet. This was a weekend outing of cycling clubs largely from the Tyneside area. Each cyclists' club seems to have adopted, or been adopted by, a public house as its base for the weekend. The Excelsior, the Barnard Castle Cycling Club, used The Star as its base. Now the building is the Bread Oven in Horsemarket. The premises were decorated, with a prize going to the best display. On the right of this group is Peter Jackson, one of the great names of the Meet and of cycling in the town. Those cobbles must have been dreadful to ride over.

Whit Monday, Galgate. Could the fuel have been acquired over lunch-time in one of Barney's many pubs?

With the Help of an Engine

Whether it got you there or not may have been a different matter.

An aeroplane down on the Demesnes in March 1917, only eleven years after the first flight by the Wright brothers at Kittyhawk, would be quite an event. Most Teesdale people would not have seen a plane in the air, or even on the ground. Thus it is no wonder quite a lot of photographs were taken, and have survived. The plane was a Reconnaissance Experimental 8, or an RE8, but known throughout the Royal Flying Corps as a Harry Tate. He was a famous comedian of the time, and airmen considered the plane could only have been designed by a bunch of jokers. It had an airspeed rather less than a strong wind, drank petrol, and was an aero-disaster. On this day it had left Newcastle to fly to Leeds, but it ran out of fuel at Barnard Castle. Enough said.

Tales of doom and disaster on the seventh are doubtless still told in the nineteenth hole at Barney Golf Club when flying things land in the wrong place. This fine mess happened in 1922, before the site had been incorporated in the golf course. You can still spot the location if you look carefully at the background. The plane was a Scout Experimental 5a, built at Cardington. A forced landing on unknown ground with a heavy engine at the front end made a somersault almost inevitable. So far as is known the crew walked out.

A crash which proved fatal to all on board. On 20 June 1939 a de Havilland Rapide left York bound for Newcastle with John Crouch, the king's jockey. There was bad visibility over Teesdale, and all three on board were killed when the plane hit Dora's Seat north of Newbiggin. The policeman to the rear of this picture was well known in the dale where he spent most of his career. Who remembers Big Matty?

An accident on Bowes Moor, 1907. Presumably the odd stage coach had come to grief on this road, but even with this sort of smash it still took over eighty years before the powers-that-be did anything about it. Now if only the engineers of the Roman army who laid the road out originally had still been around . . .

The same road, seventy years later, before the villagers lost patience and blocked the road themselves. Thanks to the bypass at least we don't see this sort of scene in Bowes today.

Some people tried to keep the road in decent shape, when they weren't leaning on their brushes in the time-honoured fashion. How did the driver of the steamroller keep his collar white in what must have been a pretty mucky job, or was he dressed for the picture? This was taken near Startforth between the wars.

The village bus comes along, between the wars. Very often they were one-man businesses. In many cases the men had their first experience of motor vehicles as soldiers in the First World War and started their businesses from scratch. Whether this was the case with Jack Stapleton I know not, but he built the bodywork himself at Hutton Magna, and opened up the Barningham to Darlington route with 'The Pride of the Road'. Names on buses seem to have been not uncommon. There was also the TQ, or 'Teesdale Queen' in the upper dale, though it ventured down to Barney on market days.

Lunedale once had its own garage, Raine's, at Nettlepot, but fire put an end to its career. The state of the road and the strength of tyres is apparent from the fact that even the sidecar is carrying a spare wheel.

Winston is one of the smaller villages of Teesdale, but never mind; when a steam engine broke down, sleeves were rolled up at the forge and they put it right.

The railway lines through Teesdale were
part of the famous Stockton & Darlington
Railway Company. Following Dr Beeching
there is less and less to see as the years pass.
(Fortunately rail enthusiasts are great
collectors of photos.) The upper picture
shows the viaduct across the Tees just west
of Barnard Castle in 1916. To enable
heavier trains to be worked an extra girder
was inserted. The riveters came from
Glasgow and at least two stayed, giving us
two new names in Barnard Castle,
McGreehin and Tavendale. The lower
picture shows the last days of Catcastle
viaduct over Deepdale, c. 1970. Both
bridges carried enormous loads through two
wars, a credit to Sir Thomas Bouch, the
engineer who built them, but who is more
often remembered for the ill-fated Tay
Bridge. 'The evil that men do lives after
them, the good is oft interrèd with their
bones.'

Railways abounded in filthy jobs which the photographer rarely went near. Painting a girder bridge on a windy day must have taken some beating. This cheery lot were painting the Catcastle viaduct in 1924.

The signal box at the Harmire crossing in Barnard Castle. The site is now part of Glaxo Laboratories. Their staff restaurant is called 'The Crossings'. The rails are still under the road, as was seen during the summer of 1994 when the factory entrance was being re-aligned.

SECTION FIVE

Teesdale's Mainly Farming

The farmer has probably seen the changes brought about during the last hundred years more closely than most. One thing has not changed, getting up to feed and milk stock on a cold, dark, wet, windy, Christmas morning. But the new camera is still in its box, waiting for the sun to shine.

Very occasionally a picture turns up which really does record history and the passing of an age. This is such a one. The land in this photograph was once measured in carucates, a measure of land ploughed by an ox team. Hutton Hall is referred to in the Domesday Book. For nine hundred years these fields were the province of oxen and then horses. One day in the 1950s the tractor arrived; for the first and last time horse and tractor worked land in the same field at the same time; and thank goodness Harry Hodgson got his camera out.

Farmers must be the most ingenious of men. They've got to be when the bank manager thinks they are there for his benefit. This Ingleton farmer is using a harrow which has already seen service as a gate, while George Alderson of Hutton Magna is remembered as being a dab hand at modifying old lorries into tractors.

The most boring job on the farm must surely have been hoeing turnips – a job frequently done by itinerant travelling workers, who, if on piece-work, could get to the end of a row and at least count a few more coppers. Here at Dyson House, Smallways, it is being done by the family. They must have welcomed the precision drill and selective weedkillers.

Now here, also at Dyson House, is a job that was much more interesting. Hay, until it was needed during the winter, or corn, until threshing day came round, needed some sort of a cover that was rainproof but not airtight. Unlike the house thatch, it would only need a life of about six months, so was much lighter. The bale and the combine have taken this job from the farmer.

Clipping day brought the camera out. There are lots of shearing photos, particularly around Middleton. I wonder if the tourist may have been responsible. The upper picture here, at Crossthwaite, is unusual in that it shows something of the scenic setting of the farm.

This is a family album shot taken at East Browson Farm shortly after the war by Janet Plews. Her sister and father are using a clipping machine of a type more often used for clipping horses; the father provides the skill, the daughter, turning the handle, provides the power. This is probably a unique picture.

No excuse for putting in two similar pictures other than because he or she who is not old enough to have had their tea in a Teesdale hayfield just has not lived. The reasons are endless: no clattering stinking tractor, and the few bits of horse-drawn machinery are standing silent. Why did tea made half an hour earlier and kept in a galvanized can taste so good? The smell of hay with lots of plants other than grasses in it; scones with jam; gooseberry tart and rhubarb tart. But also of course as a small boy I hadn't had a long hard day's work in the field.

Happy days. A picture from Tom Dent's family album of the Birkett children at West Park in Baldersdale. Of all the activities on the farm the hayfield was the one for children. You were never too young to try, as the cut-down rakes show. You were probably less use than you imagined, but it was a memory to treasure for the rest of your days.

Sweeping hay at Mickleton in the 1930s. All children like a ride, and standing on the back rail of a hay sweep was fairly safe. Carrie Raine is wearing the white cotton gloves which most ladies in the hayfield wore to prevent blisters and sore hands when using ropes and wooden rake handles for hours on end.

The wing sweep was the more usual type used for hay in the dale, and the odd one, or bits of one, can occasionally be found blocking a hole in a fence. Action shots with a box camera were not common, but the picture above shows that a load of hay has just been dropped at a new stack and the hauling chain is being reconnected to one of the wings of the sweep. The lower photo shows a paddy sweep. Both pictures come from the Bowes area.

During the last fifty years the hayfield has changed from an operation with the whole family involved, and virtually everything done by hand, to a completely mechanized situation where the bale of hay can only be moved by a tractor. Here at East Browson Farm near Dalton we have the halfway stage in the 1950s. The bale of hay was not too heavy for a man to lift, but to get a reasonable load on to a trailer needed an elevator. Bales were usually gathered by hand into batches of a dozen or so, and were then partly showerproof. Care and skill were needed. That load was pretty unstable, particularly if the bales were soft; and farm tracks are not the smoothest going.

Imagine the scene: 'If you think I'm going, in my working clothes, to hold your tup while it has its photo taken, then you've got another think coming. You can just wait till I get changed.' Most pictures of tups are pretty dull to the non-expert. Mrs Dent of Lunedale makes this one special.

A photo taken at the Great Yorkshire Show of Barney Mart personalities on a day out. Only Jack Walker would stand between a young bull and a wall drinking a cup of tea. One of the market characters of the 1950s, Jack had been a submariner during the war but became one of the best hands at dressing animals for showing. A heavy consumer of liquor, he successfully kicked the habit. A strong man indeed.

Farm sales must be one of the saddest events in the countryside. They mark the end of a lifetime, often many lifetimes, of damn hard work, 365 days a year in all weathers. But the time comes when there is not another generation to carry on, or worse the farm just does not produce a living income; worst of all is bankruptcy. At least it was a beautiful winter day for the Church Farm sale at Winston in 1916. Let's hope some of the neighbours bid a few items up to a daft price to give a bit of cheer to the vendor.

An enormous haystack by Teesdale standards, a great crowd of workmen and no ladies. There must be many more workers out of sight to keep that stack supplied with hay. I found that Lunton Hill at Woodland had been the farm of the colliery manager. These must surely be miners then, helping to get hay in for the pit ponies.

Peat is still cut for fuel in the Western Isles and the Shetlands. I don't know of any being cut in Teesdale, though the odd peat spade is probably to be seen in a farm shed. John Henry Alderson and his father cut some at Spital during the miners' strikes between the wars.

Farmers faced war in a different way to other folk. They still had shortages of materials and were told what to grow by a bureaucracy of very doubtful ability. But at least they could keep a pig and a few hens, and thus were cushioned a little from the food shortages the townspeople suffered. Jane and John, brother and sister, are here beside the fire at Egg Pot in Forest. A typical farmhouse range of the 1930s or '40s, with side oven and side boiler, to be blackleaded regularly. On the wall above Jane's head is a portrait of a soldier, her husband Ralph, who died a prisoner in the First World War. And this is Ralph on the right.

The cattle market in Barnard Castle is just behind the main street, but until the turn of the century cattle and sheep were sold in the main street, Galgate. Philip Langstaff of Stainton Hill Farm must have been pretty proud of this lot to have got one of the Barney photographers out to take their picture. They seem to be Wensleydales, a rare breed today. Philip is in the centre of the group, leaning on his stick, quietly waiting for the photographer to finish. But the same man below on his daughter's wedding day is right out of his depth. The sooner it's over and he can get back to his sheep the better.

The agricultural shows grew out of the need to feed a growing population and a scientific approach to farming which was developing in the eighteenth century. They were also a social occasion like the old fairs, a day off for country folk. One in Teesdale has disappeared in my lifetime: Middleton. Hury, High Force, Winston (above) and Barnard Castle (below) did not survive long into the twentieth century. The Barney Show was held in the grounds of Spring Lodge, the home of the Watson family. I have heard that the present-day annual gardening show is its descendant.

Two more village shows which are now defunct. The upper picture is of Baldersdale Show, although some pictures say Hury Show; I presume they were one and the same. The lower photo is of the High Force Show. Pictures of these long-gone shows are fairly rare, these two and the ones opposite are the only ones I've come across, and I have only seen one other, of High Force.

If you look around the farms in the Bowes area, you will see that a number of them have a similar large barn, built to a pretty high standard. The farms were all once part of the Gilmonby Estate of the Dugdales, and the barns date from the turn of the century. Here we see one of the roof trusses going up at Greta Farm, then tenanted by the Walker family. A vertical pole is used to raise the truss at a slight angle to the building. Once clear of the wall top, after a twist of a few degrees it can be lowered into place. Nowadays a large mobile crane would need to be brought umpteen miles to do a few minutes' work. That's progress.

Around the Village

In most villages there are only one or two people who can remember 1914.
Listen while you can.

Romaldkirk Village Green, before 1914 judging by the children's clothes. Look more closely. What is the hammer doing half-way up the tree? The lady seems to be wearing pantaloons; a man with well-polished boots is riding a tiny donkey; and three men are playing quoits beside the village pump. A caravan with a chimney at the rear looks as if it is made of tarred tarpaulin. Could the photograph be the work of a travelling photographer with his caravan darkroom? Does the name Alan Ramsden ring a bell with any reader?

Aldbrough is on the very edge of Teesdale, but this picture gives an indication of village life before the advent of the motor car. Didn't the cows go wandering off?

The Cathedral of the Dales, Romaldkirk, on Fair Day. A few pictures survive, most showing a much busier scene than this. Things seem to have got a bit out of hand, and the fair was eventually discontinued.

Bowes village pump in the late 1920s. A pretty informal picture or the girls would not have had their clogs on (you don't see clogs on school group photos). We know who they are so here goes, left to right: Hilda Heaviside, Beattie Donald, Doris Salkeld, Amy Nicholson, May Tewer, Jessie Scott, Millie Nicholson, Ethel Donald, -?-, Annie Clark, Marjorie Haygarth.

Romaldkirk seems to have been a hive of life and activity, but now it has no shop, no school and nearly had no post office. Tommy Oliver was postman, huntsman and drove a bus. At one time there was a thriving drama club.

The Reading Room is not enormous but the Tees Valley Beagles had their hunt ball there. When Pat Chipchase got married the Hunt turned out with an Honour Guard. Leaving the Rose and Crown on a hunting morning they seem a pretty cheerful cross-section of the village. No cars or horses here, so the odds must have been in favour of the hare.

These three pictures and a number of others of the Beagles have come from *Northern Echo* photos which have survived in Tommy's family album.

Hutton Magna, one of the smallest villages in the dale, has a history taking it back to the Domesday Book. The church lych gate reveals another record, an appalling loss for its size in the First World War. But they got going again and by the forties there was a ladies' cricket team. They were well organized, with the men doing the rolling of the pitch (see below). There were also a men's cricket team and a quoits team.

The blacksmith was vital to the economy of a village, particularly in his role as farrier. Everything would soon have ground to a halt without horseshoes. In the Hutton and Newsham area one is tempted to think it might have come to a halt without the Hind family! Jack and Ralph are outside Newsham forge in about 1913, and the notice over the door says 'HIND'S Shoeing Forge and General Blacksmith'.

There was cause for celebration in Barningham on 13 September 1913, so why not hold a special sports day on the main street? Everybody joins in from someone's grandma to a stray dog. The cause of all the fuss was a wedding in the Todd family.

Opening of Golf Course, Aug 10th 1910. 2.
Bp Auckland & Middleton Teams.

A match with Bishop Auckland marked the opening of Middleton Golf Club, 10 August 1910. It was a nine-hole course on Tarn's allotment under the shadow of Kirk Carrion – a far cry from Augusta, Georgia. Unfortunately the club didn't survive the First World War. (Barnard Castle Club will celebrate its centenary in 1998, and so far I have more pictures of Middleton's four than of Barney's one hundred years.)

Who remembers the Copper Kettle Tea Room in Cotherstone? This picture dates from the late 1940s.

A village is frequently connected for generations with the fortunes of one family; thus Lartington with the Witham family from about 1700 to 1897. Although they lived into the era of the camera, so far I've only come across paintings of them. The picture above is the earliest we are likely to see of Lartington Hall, about 1860.

Lartington Hall was the home of Mr and Mrs Norman Field for much of the mid-1900s. The car needs no introduction, but the chauffeurs are Tommy Rowe and Pat Kelly. The other three staff cannot be named, so far.

Norman Field was, for an American, rather restrained, but Olive more than made up for him. She is remembered for her enormous drive and energy, used particularly for the benefit of those in a less fortunate position than her own. The Fields' first house was given to the Red Cross as a convalescent home, then Lartington Hall became another convalescent home during the Second World War. Invalid Tricycle Association, girl guides, magistrates, all remember her with gratitude. PY 8000 was a famous number plate around Teesdale, until sadly a motor accident deprived us of a great character.

Lartington still has a High Pond and a Low Pond, but it once had a village pond, where the trees now are on the opposite side of the road to the houses. It seems a shame it has gone.

Cotherstone used to have two mills, one on the Balder, now derelict, and this one, Tees mill. What a maze of roofs; a classic case of 'it just growed'.

Bowes has, it seems, always been in the forefront of matters hydraulic. The Roman army had a simple aqueduct from Deepdale Beck to their bathhouse. In the early years of the twentieth century there was a hydro-electric power station on the River Greta to light Gilmonby Hall.

A feature of village life was the wide range of skills in a very small community. The gamekeeper was not always the most popular of men because of his duties. The skill he most needed was probably diplomacy. Here Will Allinson, the gamekeeper at Egglestone Hall, in about 1900, displays his skill at rabbit control. With knee-pads and a spit it was presumably a ferreting morning.

In Time of War

Teesdale almost completely escaped enemy action even though surrounded by army training units.

A few family photographs record occasions which turn out to be sombre events. There must have been hundreds of thousands of photographs like this one taken at some time between 1914 and 1918. In the event, this was the last picture of the family together. Mercifully the children were too young to understand.

At least they would enjoy dressing up for the peace procession in 1919. I thank Mrs Lella Eden for these two pictures of the Hird family. She is the young lady on the right in both pictures, the soldier her father. (And she is still riding round the town on a bike, albeit motorized.)

The Durham Light Infantry has always had close ties with Teesdale. Here they are shown in Horsemarket around the First World War period. (The earliest known photograph, so far, of the regiment on parade was taken in Market Place, and was published in the first *Teesdale in Old Photographs* book.)

The Leicester Regiment marching down Station Road during the First World War. This picture was taken by Skipper, one of the Barnard Castle photographers. The regimental museum was more than glad to receive the original photograph since this battalion had managed to lose many of its regimental records.

A pair of pictures which seem to have little in common. However, thereby hangs a tale. The church is at Winston and the picture in the village street was taken during the First World War. Then I was told that the airmen were a wreck recovery crew, who helped to celebrate a local wedding: Margaret Ellen Tunstall married Christopher Sayer on 1 April 1918. Those airmen are in a mixture of Royal Air Force and Royal Flying Corps uniform (ignoring the Mountie who somehow got in on the act). 1 April 1918 was the day the Royal Air Force was founded, so here we have a picture of an RAF unit 'on duty' on the day it was formed. The crash was at Station Farm, possibly the last crash of the RFC, or the first of the RAF. Much more important, though, it was Margaret Ellen's wedding day.

Woodland always takes a battering during wartime. Here is a light railway built across boggy ground at Battle Hill during the First World War to transport timber.

PEACE DAY JULY 19 1919

Eventually the tragic affair came to an end and Cotherstone celebrated.

A mere twenty-one years later and the Europeans were at it again. These are members of Winston Home Guard on a training evening.

Before Dads' Army came the LDV, the Local Defence Volunteers. Here is one of them in Romaldkirk, complete with tin hat, armband and 12-bore. Who it is I cannot say, since his pals say it is him and he says it isn't!

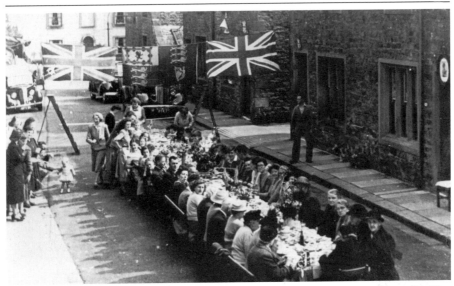

Street parties were the order of the day to celebrate the end of the Second World War. Considering that most foods were still rationed, this sort of event must have taken some ingenuity. The only picture so far to come my way is this one of Balliol Street, and even then there was some doubt about the date until someone recognized Miss Chapman taking off with mother in hot pursuit. (Ladies' hats, hemlines and ages are excellent for dating old photographs, second only to small boys with Beatles' haircuts.)

Teesdale had been full of troops for five years, but gradually the camps were run down, until now virtually all that is left is archaeology. Deerbolt is now a young offenders' institution. Here is the camp entrance, opposite the Royal Star, when the King's Royal Hussars were in residence.

No wonder your taxes are so high: if they are not losing them in the river, they are rolling them into streams. This Comet tank ended up in the beck at Streatlam during the war, while the army lorry managed to get itself into the Tees as recently as 1952. Although the culprits of the latter escapade were not discovered at the time they are slowly coming to light.

Nation of Shopkeepers

Pictures from days when turnover, or even worse, profit, per square foot was not the main criterion.

Thompson and Foster have traded from the same premises and under the same name, though different managements, for most of the twentieth century. Here we see Tommy Thompson and Harry Foster, centre, with Harry Sissons and Evelyn Allinson, obviously proud of their new shop front. For some reason it was later changed; the shop door is now to the right of the window. Note the white-painted metal rail along the front of the window; butchers' windows were open in those days and obviously measures were taken to deter street dogs from the temptation of the meat on display.

Galgate Corner – but there are a dozen corners on to Galgate. This used to be Johnson's Corner, then for most of this century it became Youngs' Corner and has now changed name yet again, to Tarn's Corner. There used to be a weighbridge in the pavement here just to the left of the shop window.

There is today only one cobbler's shop in Barnard Castle. I can personally recall five in the 1940s, and many a house had a few cobbler's tools. Here we see George Wilson standing outside his shop on the east side of The Bank before the Second World War. He later moved over the road to No. 15 where fancy goods are now sold, but when he retired about twenty-five years ago another craftsman's business, and living for a family, disappeared.

The terraced streets of Victorian towns frequently had their small family-run general shop selling almost anything. Long since having sold their last penn'orth of sweets, they can often be spotted by their shop window – now curtained. Miss Hazard (left) is outside her shop in Marshall Street in the 1920s. Later run by Mr Mitchell even through the rationing bureaucracy of the 1940s, it finally closed in the 1950s.

The Cleveland & Durham County Electric Power Company later became NESCO, then the NEEB. Now it's Northern Electric, but on a new site. Changing the name gives management something to do. The gentleman in this 1930s picture really did justify his existence, because Dick Tappin was the engineer who devised the distribution system for the scattered homes of Teesdale. If you seek his memorial look over Teesdale on a winter evening. This shop is now a hairdresser's.

Billy Kidd has reason to smile. It is the first Christmas after the war when meat is off the ration, and he has bought one of the prize animals at the Mart Christmas Fatstock Show. What more appropriate place to set up stall than on the cobbles in the Market Place, where meat has been sold for almost nine hundred years? The town shambles had been only fifty yards to his left until they were demolished in about 1804. Billy was shortly to take over a butcher's shop nearby from Harry Sayer; it is still a butcher's with a third name now, that of Keith Bellwood.

Bill's other shop was in his home village, Cotherstone, where he also had a small abattoir. This is a sad day in 1988. Cotherstone is losing its village butcher's shop. Fred Rabbitts is serving one of the last customers, Mrs Hird, with her Sunday joint, and the hooks are almost empty. Doug Hind leans on the last half-door of a butcher's shop in Teesdale, and remembers.

Sheer luck has occasionally secured a picture which may have been the only one of a particular scene. In this case I intercepted a cardboard box of photographs on their way to the saleroom, as Miss Garbutt's home was being cleared. This picture of her father Tom and an assistant must have been taken before 1933, when the present Yorkshire Bank was built. The site is now that of the hairdresser's in the Yorkshire Bank buildings. Tom's drapery business had moved from the top of The Bank to these premises in Horsemarket, then ended up just over the road where the fruit shop now stands, until his daughter Millie retired. (I put the original back in the box along with the rest, none of which were named. The rather sad remains of one of the business families of Victorian Barney.) Who is the child at the window? We'll probably never know.

Just along the street from the Yorkshire Bank was Tarn's tobacconist's and confectioner's, seen here *c.* 1920; then Mr Brown married Miss Tarn and it became Brown's the tobacconist's. What a memorable smell a tobacconist's had. Now thankfully the pernicious weed has left the premises, and it has become Ken Robinson's chocolate shop. Also gone, and this time very unfortunately, is the decorative cast-iron work. Half the shops in the town had this feature until about fifty years ago; now there is only one set left. Please don't let it go.

Still a restaurant at the top of The Bank, now Beaver's. Sadly, once again the cast-iron trellis decoration has gone.

'Monkey' Watson's at the end of Marshall Street: a typical business at the start of the motor car and wireless age. Sell bicycles and the resultant tyres and tubes, sell wireless sets and charge the batteries for them, sell petrol and start mending motor cars in the rear premises, run a taxi business – so familiar in the 1930s. You will still get petrol next door, but through this shop door, which has not changed in the slightest, you can buy a woollen sweater.

As a small boy I remember Edmund Sheppard as a slightly old-fashioned man, always impeccably dressed in a dark suit with hard white collar and sober tie. He was never flustered in a shop which always seemed to be overflowing. He was the epitome of a self-made Edwardian small-town businessman who knew his trade, his staff and his customers. The premises are now occupied by Partners.

Let's not miss the opportunity to point out that the Co-op idea did not start in Rochdale in 1844, as the cornflake packet on my table tells me, but in Middleton in January 1842. They had been on the go for over sixty years when this picture was taken.

Just along the street from the Co-op is the shop which used to be Gowland's. A shop then with rather an unusual mix, drapery and a taxi business. The present proprietors don't run a taxi service.

Give Us a Smile

The camera has proved a super way of recording the activities of groups of friends and neighbours.

The building at the bottom of Barney Bank, now the Labour Exchange or whatever they are calling it this week, was originally built as a Church of England mission. Very little survives of their activities but round about 1914 they turned out a pretty smart-looking football team.

I do not know how many people are employed by Woolworths today but in the 1940s Janet Gray, the manageress, in the centre of the second row, got all her staff together on the roof of the shop and had a photo taken.

A young lady called Bainbridge emigrated from Newbiggin to Canada just after the First World War. A couple of years ago a lady called Mrs Mewhort rang me to say she had some pictures to give me. Miss Bainbridge and Mrs Mewhort were one and the same, and the photographs from Toronto had returned to Teesdale. A couple of dozen examples from her family album, some of which are now in Newbiggin Chapel collection, included this beauty. What on earth did Middleton Bachelors' Club get up to except ensure their own disintegration as a club? Did they hold a wake each time a member fell from the straight and narrow?

Industries come and go, and some leave very little trace. The North of England Chamois Leather Company was for decades a significant employer in Barnard Castle. They made industrial gloves and a few dress gloves. I still have two pairs made forty years ago. Their factory has now been converted into three super houses by the river. This 'happy days' picture taken in the early 1950s is the only one to turn up so far with any reference to the firm.

The end of the war in 1945, and the return of men, and women, from the Forces was the occasion for a sharp growth in youth activity, frequently associated with the church or chapel. Amateur drama, particularly in the pantomime tradition, kept us off the streets on winter evenings, as rehearsals took up much of the winter. The Parish Church team, above, and the Methodist team, below, both gave shows for many years of friendly rivalry. At least one young lady here is in the wrong group . . . had a bit of talent-spotting been going on ?

Works outings seem to be a thing of the past. Presumably this is another effect of car ownership. Between the wars the staff of the *Teesdale Mercury* had a day out to the Lakes.

The word unique is regularly misused, but I would claim that a few of my photographs are unique, that is without like or equal. Six Bowes May Queens got together for a picture; they had kept their dresses and hats, had their bouquets made afresh, and had a photo taken. They are Greta Walker (1924/5), May Newbold (1926), Vera Robinson (1927), Connie Collinson (1928), Ida Walker (1929), and Edna Hind (1930).

When he had finished his butcher's round with his horse and cart, Roy Walton took on a different role as the producer of Romaldkirk Players.

E.W. Boxall is remembered by older dalesfolk as the *Darlington & Stockton Times* reporter in the dale with a penchant for large-brimmed black hats. You couldn't miss him; there he is on the edge of this photograph. He also tried his hand at writing a historical pageant set in the castle grounds. Some of the surviving pictures, unfortunately of very poor quality, seem to indicate a tendency to the melodramatic. Whose top shelf has a copy of the script?

A picture which caused a merry dance. It's another Yeoman, but no-one seemed to know what or when. Then Jim put it in the *Mercury* and by the time I was half-way down the street on Wednesday morning I'd been told it was Barnard Castle Freemasons on an outing to Valence Lodge near Langdon Beck, pre-1914. Most of the names were known, there was a copy on the wall of the local lodge and, just to put me in my place, the portly gentleman on the extreme right of the front row was my own great-grandfather.

Now here is a picture which is still defying elucidation. It is certainly taken outside the Lead Company School in Middleton. It is the 2nd (Volunteer) Battalion of the Durham Light Infantry, and the gentleman on the left is possibly Lt. Metcalf Gibson, from comparison with other pictures in the Regimental Museum at Durham. There the story sticks. Help.

Another of the pictures which have been to Canada, but which came back without a caption on the back. Then Mary Lowes applied her knowledge of the upper dale to the problem, with the result that we now know that it is a picture taken outside the school at Newbiggin on the occasion of Queen Victoria's Diamond Jubilee.

Barnard Castle First XI in 1936. One couldn't imagine 'dirt' in these trouser pockets for burnishing cricket balls. Roy Watson, one of the great names of Barney Cricket Club, is wearing his Barnard Castle School Old Barnardian Colours. Who else, like the author, remembers being paid a tanner a bucketful for digging daisy and dandelion plants out of the cricket field? A similar monetary consideration applied to boys singing in the church choir. It is not too late to recognize that Roy's hand went into his pocket for both these causes.

No book of copies of old photographs must miss the school group. These pictures have, I reckon, the greatest 'ooh aah' factor of the lot when old and not-so-old friends meet. Above we have Winston School and below Wycliffe – both in the mid- to late twenties and both now closed. The teacher at Winston is Mr Tom Watson, while at Wycliffe Miss Blanche Wellburn is in charge, and that's all the help I'm giving you.

Village life, summer and winter. The crowning of the May Queen at Boldron, not so long ago, and (below) the Christmas pantomime at Bowes. Now, that lot have hidden behind their make-up long enough, so stand up Keith Donald, Arnold Kipling, Eric Bayles, Wilf Atkinson, Geoff Atkinson, Jimmy Hemming and Mervyn Close. The part of Snow White was played by Miss Phyllis Guy.

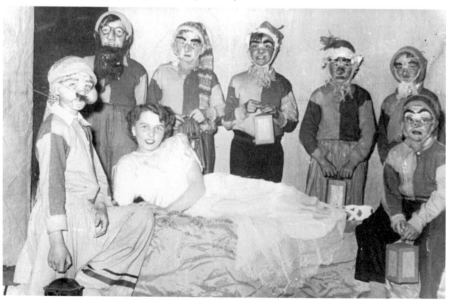

SECTION TEN

Church and Chapel

The circular churchyard at Stanwick may be a relic of a pre-Christian site, while a hay shed across the river is all that is left of the Holwick Mission Church. Sunday School and Youth Group photographs tell of a time when *East Enders* and computer games were not the limit of a child's thoughts.

Pictures are often connected completely by chance. These two are of Sunday School outings. They are both taken on the platform of Cotherstone station, long since closed by Beeching. The older one, probably, judging by the ladies' hats, some time before 1914, shows Cotherstone Sunday School children setting off, almost certainly for Redcar, on their annual outing. The second picture is on the same station platform, but in the middle of the Second World War Sunday School trips to the seaside had to be abandoned. Not to be beaten by Hitler, the Wesleyan Sunday School in Barnard Castle went on a picnic to Cotherstone, all of 4 miles away. I trust they knew where they were, for as the empty posts show the station name had been removed so that Adolf wouldn't know where he was if he turned up uninvited.

Some years ago, while putting together an album of photographs of long-gone churches and schools in the upper dale, I heard of the tin mission church at Holwick. There is not even a crop mark left on site. Then Clarrie Beadle, one of the chapel experts in Upper Teesdale, said, 'Nip down to West Brockersgill and see Sylvia Richardson.' Sure enough, Sylvia and her husband have the remains doing sterling service as a hay shed, but more to the point she produced a couple of pictures: Harvest Festival and her grandfather, Mr Fred Shield, on a horse, with the mission church in the background. Now who is going to produce for us a picture of the Lunedale Mission Church ?

The girls of Barnard Castle Congregational Sunday School giving a display of flag waving in the 1920s.

The Sunday School movement has been an introduction to drama and getting up in public for many a youngster, but the production these young ladies were presenting in the Barnard Castle Congregational Sunday School in about 1916 would seem to have been a bit of a trial to modern ears. The play was called *Discomfited Peggy and How She Was Cured*.

The Ebenezer Chapel congregation at Forest, 1907. A group where inevitably only one or two names are known today. They are most likely to be celebrating the hundredth anniversary of the Mow Cop disruption. This event, named after a village on the Cheshire/Staffordshire border, was where a group of Wesleyan worshippers broke away from the main tradition and founded the Primitive Methodists.

The tiny chapel in Holwick. It even had terraced seating at one end. It has now had two garage doors put in, so Holwick has lost chapel, church and school.

The Methodists have always had a great following among miners, lead and coal. Here we are on Cockfield Fell, at a camp meeting, on the first Sunday in July in the 1950s. The tumbled nature of the site betrays the history of the fell, going back almost to the days when the man they are praising was walking the fells of Palestine. In a Durham pit village even a chapel service doesn't get far away from a pigeon cree. How did they get that piano across that ground, and keep it in tune?

A miserable-looking day in Newgate – but a picture which, while very faded, has a lot of detail. Buildings which have now gone can be seen, and one has been built and demolished since the time of this photograph. The spire on the left was that of the Unitarian Chapel, built in 1870; thus an earliest date for the picture. You can just make out the straight line of the cottages beyond, the first of which went in 1933/4 to give a better access to The Bank from Newgate. The chapel became the Church Institute, then gave way to the present parish hall in the 1950s. The lower arrow gives the hole in the wall exit, which proves the picture was taken before 1887, when the Methodist Chapel was built; it has now also been replaced by flats. The ironwork and statues on Borrowdale's shop survived until the mid-twentieth century. This must be one of the oldest buildings in Newgate. There is evidence in its construction that it originally faced along Newgate rather than across the street.

A picture does not have to be old to be historic. All that is left standing of this Primitive Methodist Chapel is its foundation stone, which is built into a smart new block of flats. The sight of the communion rail and pulpit being used as a hardware store must be sad for those who worshipped there; even more so for those married at that rail.

The Sunday School Procession of Witness was a high spot of the year. Here we see the Barnard Castle procession coming along Horsemarket on its way to the Scar Top, sometime around 1900.

On the court, c. 1947. The younger folk of the Methodist Chapel had their own tennis court, where the girl guide hut now stands. (In the parish church youth club we had a deal with the vicar, Alan Webster: for keeping the vicarage lawns in order we could use the tennis court most evenings.)

Inside the Ebenezer Chapel in Forest just before its closure in the 1980s.

Stanley Ireland looks sadly at Harwood Chapel, 1990. The blue gentians are in bloom across the road, but inside there is only the echo of a Methodist hymn.

A name like Bede Kirk would surely hint at an ecclesiastical origin. That was the name of the small group of buildings in Harmire Road where the police station now stands. Sure enough, when the bulldozers moved in the case was proven, and the evidence destroyed except for a few photographs.

St Mary's Parish Church bellringers in the 1950s. Children should be seen and not heard, but Ernie Willis and his team were heard but seldom seen together. With a full team the tower declaimed across the town, 'No Bells Can Ring Like Our Bells Can'. Not to be outdone, the steeple of Startforth just over the river retorts, 'We Can, We Can'.

A Roof Over Your Head

Planning causes endless debate, particularly in small towns. At the end of the day I suppose it is about what our surroundings look like and how we would like them to look.

Dobson's Tripe Shop in Bridgegate. This picture was taken by Atkinson, a Barnard Castle photographer of the last century. The building survived until the 1950s, but with a tiled roof. Here we appear to have a turf or heather thatch. It seems remarkable that a thatch survived so long in the town. Surely Mr Atkinson took the photograph because it was the last thatch in Barnard Castle! Two Barnard Castle ladies remember their uncle, whose shop it was. Note again the half-door on the butcher's shop.

The Red Lion in Cotherstone kept its thatch until the 1930s, while Freewill House at
Briscoe (below) is now a ruin.

Teesdale is an area with abundant good building stone, both for walls and roofs. Brick and thatch were not greatly used. One thatch at Levy Pool survived until a few years ago. The picture above was taken in Hunderthwaite, that below in Cotherstone.

This Cotherstone house with its classical Doric door surround and baroque-style lintels was probably built in the late 1700s. About a hundred years ago it was replaced by Nicholson Terrace.

This substantial-looking house lasted a mere fifty years. All that is left now is its name, incorporated in Sherwood Close. It was the home of Dr Robinson.

Peels Yard, off Bridgegate in Barnard Castle. These yards, while probably not so bad as those in the industrial cities and the rookeries of London, were still pretty grim by 1994 standards. The description of them in the Ranger Report after the 1847 and 1849 cholera outbreak makes horrific reading. By the time these pictures were taken in the late 1940s at least the tanning pits, the pigsties and the earth closets had gone; the main cause of the trouble, overcrowding, was still there. These are examples of scenes which were rarely photographed and are only here because family snapshots have come my way; the viewfinder on the box Brownie was so poor that we often got more background than people. The upper picture was taken with the photographer's back to Bridgegate; the lower is of the same yard looking the opposite way, from a different family album.

Miles Bainbridge and a neighbour with a couple of Swaledale tups outside his home, Bink House, *c*. 1900. The farm is now beneath Selset reservoir.

An idyllic setting for a house. This is the Wycliffe boat house where the ferry crossed the Tees just below Whorlton suspension bridge.

The upper of these pictures is a fairly well-known one of Newgate Corner before the building of Barclays Bank. The lower one has only come to light in 1994. Taken by Kipling, one of the very early Barnard Castle photographers, it survives as a *carte de visite* (a mere 3 in by 2 in). It was taken from the top of The Bank and appears to show some of the buildings on the upper picture during their demolition in preparation for the building of Barclays Bank.

SECTION TWELVE

And So to School

If your regulation mug shot taken at school is no better than mine then it is best forgotten. So we'll have none of them in this section.

This timber school building was up Kelton Road about half a mile out of Mickleton. All that is left of the school building today is half a dozen brick courses (the base of the original fireplace) in a field 5 yd off the road west of Kirk View. I assume the timber, and thus temporary, school was put up to cater for the families of reservoir construction workers on Grassholme. It also saved a young lady from West Pasture from having to walk all the way down to Mickleton, at least for her first year or two at school. The young lady is now Mrs Betty Lowson of Egglestone.

So-called progress has seen the closure of many dales schools. One of the most remote in Teesdale was that of Harwood, which had the blackboard cleaned for the last time in 1947. It is now just a ruin. The dancing team is from the late 1930s. Let's give them a credit: Eric Hodgson, Richard Bayles, Thomas Rumney, Cecil Jackson, Wilfred Summerson, Ernest Dowson, William Watson and John Robinson (who supplied the snapshot).

Here is the same school in about 1916. The concert party is with the head, Mr Weedy, his wife and daughter.

How many men started a lifelong interest in gardening on a school plot (apart from a few who started a lifelong dislike of it)? Here we have the lads of Startforth school in the mid-twenties with Boss Bailey.

School groups are pretty common in the family photograph collection. Christmas concerts and Nativity plays occasionally turn up, the camera sometimes appeared on sports days, but very rarely for normal class activity. I have, however, a pair of photographs from Winston School just before it closed down in the 1950s. They are both of a PT class. They seem to have been posed, but none the less this was PT, or gym as it was usually called before the days of fancy equipment. The premises are now The Bridgewater Arms.

Elijah Yeoman

Elijah Yeoman was born in Middleham and came to Barnard Castle as a very young man to start a photographic business in 1864. He first appears living in Marshall Street with his wife and an apprentice or assistant. Eventually his business premises were in Galgate where Addison's the estate agents now are. He had a branch in Kirkby Stephen and another in Hartlepool, where the business eventually ran under another name. There is no wonder that he succeeded: he was a perfect craftsman, as his surviving prints demonstrate, and he had an excellent eye for a picture. Sadly none of his negatives have survived, unless some are hidden away in an attic.

Of the four or five photographers working in Barnard Castle he is the only one to have left us a selection of what might be called exhibition prints. These are scattered in private houses and the Bowes Museum, where there are usually a few on display. Kipling and Sinclair have left us a lot of postcards of local events and street scenes, but all three and a number of other photographers seem to have made their living largely from portraits. Most of Yeoman's scenic pictures are sepia-toned, and not a few are platinum prints, a process at which he was a master.

E. YEOMAN,

Under Royal Patronage.

Established 1864.

PHOTOGRAPHER.

Telephone No. 30.

This portrait, advertising Yeoman's service, is taken from an undated town guide/brochure. Most of the other photographs in the brochure were also taken by him. This portrait of a very self-confident young man cannot so far be identified. The Bowes-Lyon family have been ruled out, though he did take photographs at Streatlam and Raby, hence the royal patronage cachet. There is a picture showing Edward VII and his queen at Raby. The young Lady Elizabeth Bowes-Lyon spent some of her childhood holidays at Streatlam, so let's hope some of Elijah's pictures are now in Clarence House.

Streatlam Castle, demolished in the 1950s. It had been the home of the Bowes family since the Middle Ages, though the building shown here dates from around 1700. Sir George Bowes was living in the previous building when the rising in the north was being plotted by the Border earls in the castle at Raby just a couple of miles away. (The plan was to put Mary Queen of Scots on the throne of England and to restore the Roman Catholic Church to supremacy.) Sir George left home and went to the more defensible Barnard Castle, where he held out for eleven days against the rebels. It is from this event that the local skipping song arises: 'Cowardy, Cowardy, Barney Cassel, Daren't come out and fight a battle.' Sir George made a couple of sorties during the siege, though by sitting tight he gained sufficient time for a reaction from London and York which ended with the failure of the rising and the exile or execution of the main rebels. Many lesser fry were indicted for treason and some ended on the local gallows. During Sir George's absence at Barnard Castle, Streatlam was of course sacked by the rebels.

Another Yeoman picture of Streatlam Castle to complete the story. Eventually the wealth of the Bowes family, based on Teesdale landowning and Durham coal, and Scottish nobility from Glamis in Angus (Macbeth's home), was joined in marriage to give us the Bowes-Lyons. Then a servant girl from Stainton catches the eye of the Earl of Strathmore, and we have John Bowes. (If you like romance, his parents only married the day before his father died.) A French actress, Josephine Coffin-Chevallier, appears on the scene, John marries and we get one of the finest museums and art collections in Britain built in Teesdale.

No book of pictures of Teesdale can be without a Bowes Museum photograph, so let's do the job properly with one by the finest photographer the dale has seen. This view dates from when Josephine's monkey puzzle tree was a mere sapling, the Roman Catholic Chapel had been started, and the central pond was still an ornamental pond before the bandstand had been built.

Another house with strong John Bowes connections, Wemmergill Hall.

The railway line on the top of Stainmore on a winter's day, and in summer the same line as it crosses the river over Tees viaduct. A small number of straightforward industrial photographs by Yeoman have survived.

The trees in Flatts Woods have been taken
out for timber, though they are now
growing again, so Yeoman could come and
take these pictures again today. The
Edwardian dresses lent themselves to this
type of picture, and allow us to see him at
his very best.

Two medallion photographs of Market Place and Horsemarket. You can be almost certain that if Yeoman's pictures are in a frame then they have spent the better part of a century on a wall in the sunlight. Even Elijah's quality suffers under that sort of treatment. However, it is possible to find a picture of most of Galgate, Horsemarket and Market Place as they were in about 1900, showing what one of the finest small market town main streets in England could look like.

Another Flatts Woods photograph, this time in winter. The picture was behind glass and the frame, of thin sheet brass, was crimped round the sandwich of glass, photograph and card backing. It is about 8 in by 6 in, the glass is very thin, and if broken is very tricky to deal with because it may be stuck to the print– as was the one on the previous page.

Lendings Farm just over the river from Barnard Castle. That splendid, though admittedly today rather useless, barn has now been replaced by a caravan site.

Elijah Yeoman (1846–1930).

SECTION FOURTEEN

To End Where We Began

Ye Merry Musicians of Teesdale,
Who love on the fiddle to play,
Who go unto dances and parties,
Where music and dancing hold sway;
Your music is sweet and you please us,
With many a fine melting strain;
But the best of your corps is ta'en from us
The Fiddler – brave Old Parkin Raine.

Richard Watson
Leadminer poet

(Song about author's great-great-grandfather)

Before 1914 every village seems to have had its own band, no doubt with quite a bit of deputizing, as still happens. These two pictures show Mickleton; the first showing the band on its best behaviour for a formal photograph, whereas in the second they were obviously out to enjoy themselves and make money for hospital funds.

Middleton could manage a small orchestra before 1914. This group was part of the Rechabite Chapel, a teetotal group, in marked contrast to the lower group, the Mugs Band, that keeps turning up in pictures of Middleton processions. Is the patch on each player's nose something to do with a reluctance to march past a pub? Never mind, the bands must have been great fun.

Who remembers Baldersdale Arcadians, one of the many dance bands around the dale in the 1930s? The personnel were William Addison, Nellie Addison, Joe Donald and Tommy Bousfield.

A dance band on stage in the old Mickleton Institute, 1 November 1911. Ernest Raine (post office), Thomas Raine (Bowbank) and Tommy Townson.

Bowes Band pose for a group photograph in the Vicarage garden, 1930s. Here we know all the names because Norman Scrafton is still around. So, left to right and back to front: Joe Walker, Herbert Sayer, William Parker, John Pickersgill, Thomas Layton, Peter Walker, Tom Bousfield, Edward Rowe, Norman Scrafton, William Hillery, Edward Coates, Joshua Gargett, Cecil Pickersgill, Richard Gargett, Adam Liddle and Arthur Guy (percussion).

Barney Band in front of the bandstand at the Bowes Museum. There are mixed feelings about the removal of the cast-iron Victorian bandstand – incongruous in front of a French chateau, yes, but it's a shame a home could not have been found for it somewhere nearby. So far we have not been able to name this group, but if we just call every third one Wright, we'll not go far wrong. That family probably gave the youngsters a mouthpiece rather than a dummy.

Barnard Castle Amateur Operatic and Dramatic Society, to give it its full title, presented *HMS Pinafore* as their first production in 1911, though some of the same folk had put on *Trial by Jury* the previous year. When the cinema, the Victoria Hall, put in an unmovable screen for Cinemascope, the society had to find a new home, but the other stages in the town were inadequate and the society folded. It had lasted ten times as long as Cinemascope, nearly ten times as long as bingo which followed, and one young lady in this picture outlived the whole lot – Edith Nicholson, in the pigtails, who lived till the spring of 1994.

Does the Church Lads' Brigade still exist as a youth group? This is the Barnard Castle group in about 1948. They had a bugle and drum band which I seem to remember was pretty good. Old members say that to hear the Durham County bands all together on the green at Durham Cathedral was quite something.

From the 2094 edition of *Teesdale in Old Photographs*. . . . The Teesdale Car Company provided a service to the motorist through most of the twentieth century. Early in 1993 it was pulled down and redeveloped by David Nesbitt, who was still giving a service to the motorist. In the early decades of the twenty-first century . . .

Acknowledgements

The author would like to take this opportunity to thank all those people who over the years have allowed him to copy their photographs, a tiny fraction of which appear in this book. The collection will, I trust, remain in the Bowes Museum as a source collection for so long as the materials last.

Pictures from the family collections of the following have gone into the compilation of the book.

Ladies first: Mrs E. Atkinson • Mrs E.M. Beadle • Mrs W. Beadle
Mrs E. Beere • Mrs M. Bell • Mrs G. Bonnet • Mrs G. Browning
Mrs M. Chapman • Miss Close • Mrs J. Cooper • Mrs D. Clarkson
Mrs L. Eden • Mrs I. Hall • Mrs D. Hempsall • Mrs T. Hodgson
Mrs I. Kidd • Mrs M. Lewis • Mrs B. Lowson • Mrs M. Lowson
Mrs L. Marshall • Mrs F. McGregor • Mrs P. Mewhort • Mrs G. Mitchell
Mrs P. Nixon • Mrs J. Nuttall • Miss J. Plews • Mrs S. Richardson
Miss C. Simpson • Mrs D. Taylor • Mrs R. Thompson • Mrs A. Tunstall
Mrs D. Tunstall • Mrs E. Underwood • Mrs G. Whitfield • Mrs M. Wallis
Mrs C. Wilkinson.
The gentlemen: M. Abraham • J.H. Alderson • A. Ashmore • S. Atkinson
C. Beadle • T. Beck • T. Boyd • N. Brereton • W. Cummins • C. Dent • J. Dent
B. Elliott • W. Harwood • R. Hillery • A. Howson • S. Ireland
G. McGreehin • J. Morton • L. Nelson • C. Priestley • R. Rackham
R. Raine • F. Richardson • J. Robinson • W. Robinson • D. Sheppard
B. Sparrow • G. Sparrow • A. Stoddart • N. Turner • H. Watson
E. Wilkinson • J. Winter • L. Wood.

Some of the photographs I have received from more than one source; please accept my apologies if there appears to be a missed credit.

The Bowes Museum and the *Northern Echo* are both due my thanks for allowing me to use photographs in their possession.

Denis Coggins and Alan Wilkinson have helped me avoid at least some errors, and any remaining must be my fault, while without John Yarker's specialist knowledge the aeroplane page would have been very short on facts.

Thank you all.